ISBN: 9798839206472

Imprint: Independently published

GW00730655

All facts correct as of 21st July 2022

A'gas dynergh
Welcome

Here are 150 facts about the historic county and Celtic nation of Cornwall. As one of the most unique counties in the United Kingdom, Cornwall has faced a history of oppression through the centuries and has fought life and death to keep its autonomy. Many elements of its distinct culture have survived until this day and you will learn all about this culture, history and much much more in the following pages.

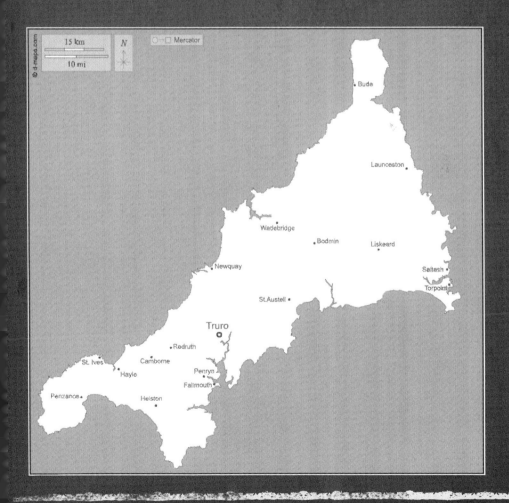

1. The Cornish pasty has had Protected Geographical Indication (PGI) status in Europe since 2011.

2. The Cornish Pasty Association aims to ensure this status is upheld. and raises awareness of Cornish pasties around the world.

3. The English word "pasty" derives from Medieval French for a pie, filled with venison, salmon or other meat, vegetables or cheese, baked without a dish.

4. Cornwall is called Kernow in the Cornish language.

---

5. Cornish is a revived language, having become extinct at the end of the 18th century as a living community language.

---

6. The first Cornish-language day care opened in 2010.

7. Dorothy Pentreath (1692-1777), known as Dolly, was the last known native speaker of the Cornish language and is the best known of the last fluent speakers of Cornish.

8. It is estimated that there are around 300-600 fluent speakers of Cornish today.

9. Hello in Cornish is dydh da.

10. There are over 385 types of plants in Cornwall.

_____

11. Cornwall's coastline is 433 miles long, with 300 beaches!

_____

12. Truro is the only city in Cornwall.

13. Truro became mainland Britain's southernmost city in 1876.

---

14. Truro is the third capital of Cornwall after Launceston and Lostwithiel.

---

15. Truro's cathedral was completed in 1910.

16. Truro City FC won the second-ever final at the new Wembley Stadium in 2007 by beating A.F.C Totten in the FA Vase Final.

_____

17. Cornwall's international airport is based in Newquay.

_____

18. The river Tamar forms most of the border with Devon.

19. Devon is the only county that Cornwall borders.

---

20. Cornwall has the 12th largest county in England out of 48 by area.

---

21. Cornwall has an area of 1,375 sq miles.

22. Cornwall has a population of around 560,000.

---

23. Cornwall is the 8th least populated county in England.

---

24. Cornwall is also one of the least diverse counties in England with a 95.7% white British population compared to 85.4% nationally.

25. In 875, the last recorded king of Cornwall, Dumgarth, is said to have drowned.

---

26. According to William of Malmesbury, writing around 1120, King Athelstan of England (924-939) set the border between the English and Cornish people at the east bank of the River Tamar where it remains today.

---

27. Cornwall was known to the Anglo-Saxons as "West Wales" to distinguish it from "North Wales" (the modern nation of Wales).

28. The name appears in the Anglo-Saxon Chronicle in 891 as On Corn walum. In the Domesday Book it was referred to as Cornualia and in c. 1198 as Cornwal.

---

29. The latin name for the county was Cornubia (first appearing in a mid-9th-century deed purporting to be a copy of one dating from c. 705), and as Cornugallia in 1086.

---

30. Cornwall forms the very south west tip of the island of Great Britain, and is therefore exposed to the full force of the prevailing winds that blow in from the Atlantic Ocean in the west.

31. Cornwall's border with Devon that is not defined by the Tamar is formed by the Marsland Valley.

---

32. The aptly named High Cliff, between Boscastle and St Gennys, is the highest sheer-drop cliff in Cornwall at 223 metres (732 ft).

---

33. The south coast of the county, dubbed the "Cornish Riviera", is more sheltered and there are several large estuaries such as Falmouth and Fowey that offer safe anchorages.

34. It is thought tin was mined here as early as the Bronze Age, and copper, lead, zinc and silver have all been mined in Cornwall in the past.

---

35. The Lizard peninsula has unusual geology, and is the only example in Great Britain of an ophiolite, a section of oceanic crust now found on land.

---

36. The Lizard Peninsula is home to rare plants, such as the Cornish Heath, which has been adopted as the county flower.

37. St Just in Penwith is the westernmost town in England.

---

38. Camborne is the county's largest town and is more populous than the capital Truro.

---

39. St Austell is also larger than Truro and was the centre of the china clay industry in Cornwall.

40. St Austell was the largest settlement in Cornwall until four new parishes were created for the area on the 1st of April 2009.

---

41. There are no motorways in Cornwall with the closest being the M5 near Exeter.

---

42. The Isles of Scilly are served by ferry (from Penzance) and plane from its airport in St Mary's.

43. There are regular flights between St Mary's and Land's End Airport, near St Just, and Newquay Airport; during the summer season, a service is also provided between St Mary's and Exeter Airport, in Devon.

---

44. Cardiff and Swansea in Wales have at some times in the past been connected to Cornwall by ferry, but these do not operate now.

---

45. The city of Plymouth in south west Devon is an important location for key services such as hospitals, department stores, road and rail transport, and cultural venues, particularly for people living in east Cornwall.

46. Cornwall has a temperate Oceanic climate (Köppen climate classification: Cfb), with mild winters and cool summers.

---

47. It has the mildest and one of the sunniest climates in the UK, as a result of its oceanic setting and the influence of the Gulf Stream.

---

48. The average annual temperature in Cornwall ranges from 11.6 °C (52.9 °F) on the Isles of Scilly to 9.8 °C (49.6 °F) in the central uplands.

49. The effects of the warm ocean currents make winters among the warmest in the UK. This also makes and frost and snow very rare at the coast and are also rare in the central upland areas.

---

50. Summers are, however, not as warm as in other parts of southern England.

---

51. Cornwall is one of the sunniest areas in the UK. It has more than 1,541 hours of sunshine per year, with the highest average of 7.6 hours of sunshine per day in July.

52. The moist, mild air coming from the southwest brings higher amounts of rainfall than in eastern Great Britain, at 1,051 to 1,290 mm (41.4 to 50.8 in) per year.

---

53. The Isles of Scilly has on average fewer than two days of air frost per year making it the only area in the UK to be in the Hardiness zone 10.

---

54. Extreme temperatures in Cornwall are very rare, but extreme weather in the form of storms and floods is common.

55. The Isles of Scilly have, on average, less than one day of air temperature exceeding 30 °C per year and are in the AHS Heat Zone 1.

---

56. Cornish World is a magazine covering all aspects of Cornish life and is popular with Cornish residents and descendants of Cornwall around the world.

---

57. Charles Causley was born in Launceston and is perhaps the best known of Cornish poets.

58. William Golding, the Nobel-prizewinning novelist was born in St Columb Minor in 1911, and returned to live near Truro from 1985 until his death in 1993.

---

59. The late Poet Laureate Sir John Betjeman was famously fond of Cornwall and it featured prominently in his poetry.

---

60. The English-born poet Sylvia Kantaris returned to the UK in 1971 and settled in Helston in 1974. She was appointed as Cornwall's first Writer in the Community in 1986.

61. Agatha Christie's "Poirot" short story "The Cornish Adventure" takes place in Polgarwith, a small made up market town in Cornwall.

---

62. In contrast to the situation in Wales, the churches failed to produce a translation of the Bible into the local language, and this has been seen by some as a crucial factor in the demise of the language.

---

63. A translation was eventually made in 2002.

64. Traditionally, the Cornish have been non-conformists in religion. In 1549, the Prayer Book Rebellion caused the deaths of thousands of people from Devon and Cornwall.

---

65. Celtic Christianity was an important part of Cornish life and many Cornish Saints are commemorated in legends, churches and placenames.

---

66. Methodism still plays a large part in the religious life of Cornwall today, although Cornwall has shared in the post-World War II decline in British religious feeling.

67. A campaign group formed in 2003 called Fry an Spyrys (free the spirit in Cornish) is dedicated to disestablishing the Church of England in Cornwall and to forming an autonomous province of the Anglican Communion – a Church of Cornwall.

---

68. Saint Piran's Flag, a white cross on a black background is often seen in Cornwall.

---

69. The chough (in Cornish = palores) is also used as a symbol of Cornwall.

70. "Chough" was also used as a nickname for Cornish people.

---

71. Another animal with a deep association with Cornwall is the "White Horse of Lyonesse". Arthurian legends tell of a rider escaping on a white horse as the land sunk beneath the waves, surviving and settling in Cornwall.

---

72. An anvil is sometimes used to symbolise Cornish nationalism, particularly in its more extreme forms.

73. Established in 1970, the Institute of Cornish Studies moved to the new Combined Universities in Cornwall Campus at Tremough, Penryn in October 2004: the institute is a branch of the University of Exeter.

---

74. The Federation of Old Cornwall Societies have published a series of books about Cornwall's past.

---

75. Cornwall has the highest density of traditional 'Celtic crosses' of any nation, and medieval holy wells are common.

Well done for reaching the halfway point. It's time to check you have been taking all the information in by testing your knowledge with a quick quiz! There are 10 questions, good luck!

1. What is Cornwall's capital city?

2. In what century did the prayer book rebellion take place?

3. Who was the last known native speaker of the Cornish language?

4. Who was the last King of Cornwall?

5. What is Cornwall's largest settlement?

6. What is hello in Cornish?

7. What year was a Cornish translation of the bible eventually made?

8. What is the population of Cornwall?

9. Who is the patron saint of Cornwall?

10. The River Tamar and what valley form the border with Devon?

76. Cornwall has a rich and vibrant folk music tradition which has survived into the present day.

---

77. Cornish Celtic music is a relatively large phenomenon given the size of the region. A recent tally found over 100 bands playing mostly or entirely Cornish folk music.

---

78. The most famous Furry Dance takes place in Helston and is one of the oldest British customs still practised today.

79. The Cornish and Breton languages were mutually intelligible until Tudor times.

---

80. The only known feature-length film in the Cornish language is Hwerow Hweg (Bitter Sweet), which also has an English version.

---

81. The "traditional dress" of Cornwall for women is a bal maiden's or fishwife's costume. This includes the wearing of a bonnet known as a "gook" (which were peculiar to a district or community,) aprons and woollen shawls.

82. Euchre is a popular card game in Cornwall and there are many leagues throughout the county.

---

83. For men fishermen's smocks, Guernsey sweaters (known as worsted-frocks in Cornwall) and long cut shirts are worn.

---

84. The Cornish kilt is becoming increasingly popular, and these kilts are available in various Cornish tartans or plain black.

85. The Cornish national tartan was designed by E. E Morton Nance in 1963 using colours traditionally associated with Cornwall. Fragments of tartan have been found in Penwith.

---

86. Cornish clotted cream is a popular topping on scones.

---

87. Queen drummer Roger Taylor attended school in Truro and currently lives not far from Falmouth.

88. Mick Fleetwood of Fleetwood Mac was born in Redruth.

---

89. The popular BBC series Poldark (2015-19) stories Captain Ross Vennor Poldark's return from the American War of Independence in 1873. He returns to his home of Nampara in Cornwall after three years in the army.

---

90. Tintagel Castle is reputedly King Arthur's birthplace.

91. The world pilot gig rowing championships take place annually in the Isles of Scilly.

---

92. In 2014, half of the men's GB team fenced for Truro Fencing Club, and 3 Truro fencers appeared at the 2012 Olympics.

---

93. There are many types of beers brewed in Cornwall including those produced by Sharp's Brewery, Skinner's Brewery, Keltek Brewery and St Austell Brewery.

94. Newlyn is the largest fishing port in the UK by value of fish landed.

---

95. The Isles of Scilly form part of the ceremonial county of Cornwall, and have, at times, been served by the same county administration. Since 1890 they have been administered by their own unitary authority, the Council of the Isles of Scilly.

---

96. Cornwall is divided into six county constituencies to elect MPs to the House of Commons and there was a surprising result in the 2005 general election where all of MPs voted in were Liberal Democrats.

97. On the 24th of April 2014 Cornish people were granted minority status under the European Framework Convention for the Protection of National Minorities.

---

98. The Cornish nationalist movement contests the present constitutional status of Cornwall and seeks greater autonomy within the UK.

---

99. Cornwall became part of the Brittonic Kingdom of Dumnonia after the collapse of the Roman Empire, along with Devon, parts of Dorset and Somerset.

100. It was ruled by chieftains of the Cornovii who may have included figures regarded as semi-historical or legendary, such as King Mark of Cornwall and King Arthur, evidenced by folklore traditions derived from the Historia Regum Britanniae.

---

101. After the Battle of Deorham in 577 AD, the Cornovii division of the Dumnonii tribe were separated from their fellow Brythons of Wales.

---

102. Cornwall has a population density of 410/sq mi (160/sq km).

103. Since 1337, the King or Queen's eldest son and heir has held the title of Duke of Cornwall.

---

104. Cornwall was rarely occupied during the Palaeolithic, but people returned around 10,000 years ago in the Mesolithic, after the last ice age. There is compelling evidence of occupation by hunter gatherers during this time.

---

105. The upland areas of Cornwall were the first to be settled as the vegetation required little in the way of clearance. They were likely first occupied in Neolithic times.

106. Palaeolithic remains are almost non-existent in the county.

---

107. The work of Henry Jenner sparked a revival of interest in Cornish studies in the early 20th century as well as the creation of links with the other five Celtic nations.

---

108. The late 18th and early 19th centuries were when smuggling was at its peak in Cornwall.

109. Cornwall's rugged coastline was popular with traders as a landing point looking to avoid expensive import taxes and other duties on goods.

---

110. The most trafficked items were brandy, lace and tobacco which were imported from Continental Europe.

---

111. By the 19th century, an estimated 10,000 people (most of Cornwall's population), including women and children - were participating in the smuggling business.

112. The rate of smuggling began to decline in the early 19th century and by the 1830s was greatly reduced due to better coast guarding and a reduction of excise duties on imported goods.

---

113. Devon and Cornwall were the site of a Jacobite rebellion in 1715 led by James Paynter of St. Columb.

---

114. This coincided with the larger and better-known "Fifteen Rebellion" which took place in Scotland and the north of England.

115. In 1841, there were ten hundreds of Cornwall: Stratton, Lesnewth and Trigg; East and West Wivelshire; Powder; Pydar; Kerrier; Penwith; and Scilly.

---

116. Cornwall was split into Hundreds between 925 and 1894 when it was replaced with local government districts.

---

117. All of the lordships of the Hundreds of Cornwall belonged, and still belong, to the Duchy of Cornwall, apart from Penwith which belonged to the Arundells of Lanherne.

118. Cornwall played a significant role during the English Civil War, as it was a Royalist semi-enclave in the generally Parliamentarian south-west..

---

119. An explanation for this was that Cornwall's rights and privileges were tied up with the royal Duchy and Stannaries therefore the Cornish saw the King as protector of their rights and Ducal privileges.

---

120. An Earthquake that hit Lisbon at 9:40am on the 1st of November 1755 caused a tsunami to strike the Cornish coast at around 14:00.

121. Cornwall's Lord Lieutenant since 2011 has been Colonel Edward Bolitho OBE

122. Cornwall and neighbouring Devon had large reserves of tin, which was mined extensively by people associated with the beaker culture during the Bronze Age.

123. Ingots of tin found off the coast of modern-day Israel were traced back to Cornwall from the 12th century.

124. The first account of Cornwall comes from Diodorus Siculus (c. 90 BCE - c. 30 BCE), a sicilian Greek historian supposedly quoting or paraphrasing the 4th-century BCE geographer Pytheas, who had sailed to Land's End.

---

125. The weather in Cornwall is typically 4 or 5°C warmer than the UK average.

---

126. Brown Willy in Bodmin Moor is Cornwall's highest point at 420m (1,378 ft).

127. There are approximately 75,000 cows in the county.

128. Roughly 120 million pasties are made every year in Cornwall.

129. The knotted crust of a pasty was specifically designed to use as a handle and then thrown away afterwards.

130. St Austell Brewery named after the town of the same name employs over 250 people.

131. It was founded in 1851 by Walter Hicks.

132. The brewery's flagship beer is Tribute Ale, which accounts for around 80% of sales.

133. Tribute was created to commemorate the 1999 solar eclipse and was originally a one-off special named Daylight Robbery. It proved to be so popular it was reintroduced as Tribute and has since won several awards around the UK.

---

134. Helston Garages was founded in 1960 by Mr & Mrs Carr Snr, as a filling station and repairs workshop located in the small Cornish town of the same name and now turns over £600 million a year.

---

135. The first ever Trago Mills was set up between Liskeard and Bodmin by Mike Robertson over 60 years ago.

136. Imerys is the world leader in mineral-based specialties for industry, transforming a large variety of minerals into high value specialty products using sophisticated technical processes. They employ over 1,000 people.

---

137. Tempest Photography, founded by Horace Tempest more than 80 years ago, has been at the forefront of the photography industry for nearly a century.

---

138. Warrens Bakery is Britain's oldest Cornish pasty maker, having been established in St Just in 1860.

139. Seasalt is a Cornish company specialising in women's clothing, footwear and accessories inspired by the creative and maritime heritage of Cornwall. It had a revenue of £100 million in 2021.

---

140. In 2005, Cornwall was estimated to have a GDP of 70% of the European average.

---

141. Saltash, a town in the extreme east of the county is nicknamed 'The Gateway to Cornwall".

142. Rugby Union is the most popular spectator sport in Cornwall.

---

143. Cornwall has produced many international rugby players including Phil Vickery, Trevor Woodman, Graham Dawe (England), Stack Stevens (England and British and Irish Lions) and Andy Reed (Scotland and the Lions).

---

144. The Cornish Rugby team won a silver medal at the 1908 Olympics having been chosen to represent Great Britain.

145. They lost the final to Australia 32-3 and remain the only county side to represent Team GB at the games.

---

146. Jack Nowell and Luke Cowan-Dickie, both born in Truro, were part of the England team that reached the 2019 World Cup Final and have both represented the Lions.

---

147. Cornwall have reached 13 County Championship Finals since 1989 winning 6 including 2022.

148. There are rumours of a black panther/ leopard-like that roams the moors of Cornwall and many claim to have witnessed the creature since 1978. It is commonly known as the "Beast of Bodmin Moor".

---

149. Bucca is a male sea-spirit in Cornish folklore, a merman, that inhabited mines and coastal communities as a hobgoblin during storms.

---

150. The Minack Theatre (Gwaryjy Minack in Cornish) is a striking open-air theatre built on the side of a cliff in Porthcurno, around 4 miles from Lands End.

Here is the second and final round of quiz questions based on the last 75 facts you have read. Good luck or in Cornish, chons da!

1. Until the Tudor times, Cornish was mutually intelligible with which language?

2. What card game is popular in Cornwall and has many leagues around the county?

3. Cornish-born drummer Roger Taylor is famous for being a part of which band?

4. What is the name of Ross Poldark's fictional home village in the popular BBC series?

5. Tintagel Castle is supposedly the birthplace of which mythical figure?

6. Which leading photography company is based in Cornwall?

7. What is the famous open-air theatre called?

8. Which town is nicknamed the 'Gateway to Cornwall?

9. What Olympic games did Cornwall compete in?

10. What is the name given to the mysterious black panther/leopard that is said to roam in Cornwall?

Round 1

1. Truro
2. 14th
3. Dorothy Pentreath
4. King Dumgarth,
5. Camborne
6. Dydh da
7. 2002
8. 560,000
9. St. Piran
10. Marsland

Round 2

1. Breton
2. Euchre
3. Queen
4. Nampara
5. King Arthur
6. Tempest
7. Minnack
8. Saltash
9. 1908
10. Beast of Bodmin Moor

Thank you for purchasing this Cornwall Fact Book. I hope you have enjoyed reading through and have learnt lots of interesting facts about the county.

As a small independent publisher, positive reviews left on our books go a long way to attracting new readers who share your passion for the county.

If you are able to take a few minutes out of your day to leave a review it would be greatly appreciated!

If you spot any issues you would like to raise, please do email me before leaving a negative review with any comments you may have.

I will be more than happy to liaise with you and can offer refunds or updated copies if you are unhappy with your purchase.

james.kevern25@gmail.com

—

Printed in Great Britain
by Amazon

10382217R00034